A WALK
HADF
WALL

CHARLES CHADWYCK-HEALEY

THE PENCHANT PRESS

Photographs and text ©2009 Charles Chadwyck-Healey
Designed by Geoff Green Book Design, Cambridge
Map by Tim Oliver
Printed in Great Britain by Henry Ling Ltd, Dorchester

ISBN 978 0 95437 562 1

The Penchant Press
10 North End
Bassingbourn
Royston SG8 5NX
UK

Penchant.ch@dwyck.com
Tel: 01763 245811

The photographs may also be viewed on the web at
www.dwyck.com/hadrianswall.

Acknowledgements

I would like to thank my walking companions, Andrew Shrager, Mike Prichard, Rebecca Prichard and Colin Walsh, and the authors of the books and guides from which much of the information in the captions is taken.

Amongst the most useful guides are:
Hadrian's Wall Path by Mark Richards, Cicerone 2006
Hadrian's Wall History and Guide by Guy de la Bédoyère, Tempus 2005
Hadrian's Wall Path by Anthony Burton, Aurum Press 2004
English Heritage. Hadrian's Wall by Stephen Johnson, B. T. Batsford 2004

CHARLES CHADWYCK-HEALEY

About the Book

This book brings to life the experience of walking Hadrian's Wall as it spans one of our most beautiful and unspoilt landscapes.

The photographs were taken by Charles Chadwyck-Healey, almost all on a single walk with companions in June 2006. They show the landscape, Roman forts, ancient castles and monuments, the Wall itself and the people who walk this wonderful trail. It is not a guidebook and does not attempt to include every feature on the path along the Wall.

The captions that accompany the photographs give fascinating information about the Wall and its history and about the sites that were visited on the walk.

The photographs go from East to West; from Wallsend, the beginning of the Hadrian's Wall Path National Trail, to Bowness-on-Solway, the end of the Path. Each photograph or group of photographs is located by place name; distance from Wallsend along the Path; and Ordnance Survey grid reference.

🗺 40.6 miles ⊢ NY 772682

Where the location is off the Path, two distances are given – the distance to the point at which one leaves the Path, and the distance of the detour from it.

In the Ordnance Survey grid reference the prefix letters NY and NZ refer to adjoining 100,000 metre squares.

Map of Hadrian's Wall

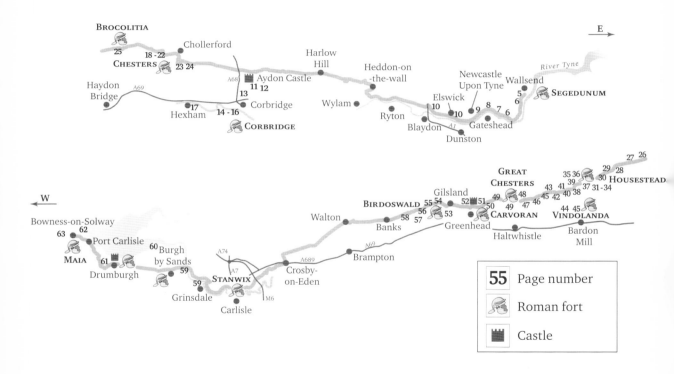

BROCOLITIA
25
18 - 22
CHESTERS
23 24
Chollerford
Harlow Hill
Heddon-on-the-wall
Newcastle Upon Tyne
Wallsend
River Tyne
E
SEGEDUNUM
5
6
Haydon Bridge
A69
A68
Aydon Castle
11 12
13
17
Hexham
14 - 16
Corbridge
CORBRIDGE
Wylam
Ryton
Blaydon
A1
Dunston
Elswick
10
10
9
8
7
6
Gateshead

27 26
GREAT CHESTERS
48
35 36
39
29 28
30
HOUSESTEAD
43 41
40 38
37 31-34
W
49
49 47 46
45 42
44 45
BIRDOSWALD
55 54
52 51
50
CARVORAN
VINDOLANDA
Gilsland
Bowness-on-Solway
63 62
MAIA
Port Carlisle
61
Drumburgh
60
Burgh by Sands
59
59
Grinsdale
STANWIX
A74
A7
M6
Carlisle
Crosby-on-Eden
A689
Brampton
A69
Walton
Banks
58 57
56
53
Greenhead
Haltwhistle
Bardon Mill

■ The Eastern end of Hadrian's Wall is on the banks of the Tyne at Wallsend. The open space is the site of the Segedunum Fort and the white-walled building houses a fine reconstruction of a Roman bathhouse with a domed and painted interior. In the 19th century miners' houses occupied the open space; now it is dominated by the cranes of the Swan Hunter shipyard. The last stones of the Wall between the river and the fort were removed in 1903 to make way for the building of the trans-Atlantic liner, the Mauretania.

Wallsend *Segedunum* +− NZ 301661

■ The first true length of Roman Wall runs West from the corner of the fort. This part of the Wall between Wallsend and Newcastle was built at a later date as an extension to the main Wall and has a width of 2 metres. The Wall was first built with a 3 metre width, the 'Broad Wall'; at a later stage, around AD 123, the width was reduced to the 2 metre 'Narrow Wall'.

■ A party of walkers rests against conveniently placed street sculptures at the junction of Quayside and St Lawrence Road in the St Lawrence district of Newcastle.

■ The 'city of bridges'. A bridge across the Tyne and a fort were built by the Romans in Hadrian's time, and were both named 'Pons Aelius', one of Hadrian's names. Later bridges were built on the same foundations. The Millennium Bridge spans the Tyne in front of the silos of the Baltic Flour Mills, which now house the BALTIC Centre for Contemporary Art. Behind it is the Tyne Bridge, completed in 1928 and designed by the firm who had designed the very similar Sydney Harbour Bridge.

Newcastle 🥾 4 miles ⊢ NZ 262641

■ The Gateshead Millennium Bridge takes pedestrians and cyclists across the Tyne to Gateshead. Opened in 2001 at a cost of £22million, it is the world's first and only tilting bridge and is both an icon and a tourist attraction. The walkway, which is supported on pivots, is raised into the air by hydraulic rams, counterbalanced by the arch from which the walkway is suspended, to allow ships to pass underneath. The posts in the water guide ships through a central channel.

Newcastle 🥾 4.4 miles ⊢ NZ 257640

■ The view from the keep of the 'New Castle upon Tyne' built in 1080 by Robert Curthouse, eldest son of William the Conqueror, on the site of the Roman fort, Pons Aelius. This was the Western end of the Wall until it was extended to Wallsend. The fort was rebuilt in the reign of Henry II, but by 1589 was described as 'old and ruinous'.

The gleaming roof of the Sage Gateshead music centre, on the far bank, is the home of the Northern Sinfonia. The building in the foreground is the Moot Hall. It replaced the old 'moot hall' of the castle and is now a Crown Court.

Newcastle 🥾 4.7 miles ⊢ NZ 252638

In the 1860s 20,000 men were employed in the Armstrong shipbuilding and armaments works and most of them lived in Scotswood. The Scotswood Road is the way to the Bladon Races in the music hall song of the same name. These Victorian brick terraces are due to be replaced with modern housing.

The river Tyne from the Riverside Walkway. The Tyne is tidal all the way to Wylam, 8 miles (13 kilometres) West of Newcastle. These are the flotsam and jetsam of a river that runs through a great city, even though the coal traffic and heavy industry that used to pollute the Tyne are long gone.

Scotswood 🥾 8 miles ⊢ NZ 204638

Elswick 🥾 5.6 miles ⊢ NZ 240629

■ The finest defended mediaeval manor house in England and the most complete 13th century house in the North. A latrine supported on stone corbels projects from the castle wall. The house was built by the de Reymes family, rich merchants from Suffolk. Edward I's warfare with the Scots led to the castle having to be fortified in 1305, but in 1315 it was pillaged and burned by the Scots and then seized by English rebels two years later. By now, de Reymes was ruined, and by the end of the 14th century Aydon was being rented out.

Aydon Castle 🥾 23.6 miles + detour 1.5 miles ⊢ NZ 002663

■ In the 16th century a new owner, Cuthbert Reynold, carried out major improvements and, by the beginning of the 17th century, Aydon was again being rented out. The castle was owned subsequently by the Douglas and Blackett families and was lived in until it was taken over by the Ministry of Works in 1966. A stone chimney flue built out from the wall can be seen on this South elevation that stands above a ravine.

■ The arch leads into the fortified inner courtyard. The main entrance is on the first floor. Grooves in the wall are evidence of a porch over the entrance door and, later, a canopy over the staircase. In the 1930s a farmer lived here alone with his animals, which were kept in the lower rooms. More recently, the castle was used in the film *Ivanhoe*.

Aydon Castle 🚶 23.6 miles + detour 1.5 miles ⊢ NZ 002663

■ The lane runs South to the town of Corbridge, near the site of Corstopitum, one of the most important Roman forts, which lies 2.5 miles (4 kilometres) South of the Wall. Until the Wall was built the frontier was represented by a track, the Stanegate, which started in Newcastle at the Pons Aelius and continued through Carlisle to the end of the Wall at Bowness-on-Solway. It ran between forts situated about every 6.2 miles (10 kilometres), including Corstopitum and Vindolanda.

■ Aydon Castle stands on the Cor Burn and the path to Corbridge runs along the burn through an enchanting wood before joining Leazes Lane.

Leazes Lane 👣 Detour 2 miles ← NY 992662

An aqueduct carried water in a closed conduit through a large aeration chamber to the right. These are the surviving walls of a stone tank that the water ran into, which was there for public use. The walls of the tank have been worn down by the overflow of the water, though it has been suggested that the wear may also have come from the sharpening of knives and tools on the stone walls.

■ Looking West across four long buildings used as workshops. There were tanks and hearths associated with iron working for making spears and arrow heads.

Five other forts are buried beneath the stone remains and the undulations are due to subsidence into the drainage ditches of the earlier forts.

Corbridge *Corstopitum* 🥾 Detour 4.1 miles ← NY 982649

■ Drainage channels run round the perimeter of the buildings and along the streets, as part of a sophisticated water supply and drainage system. The first fort was built by Agricola shortly after his victory over Scottish tribes in AD 84. The second timber fort was replaced by Hadrian, who built the third fort to house an infantry garrison.

Corbridge *Corstopitum* 🥾 Detour 4.1 miles ⊢ NY 982649

■ Looking North across one of the two granaries built in AD 140 by Hadrian's successor, Antoninus Pius, and, after interruptions, completed in the early 3rd century and in use for over 100 years. By this time Corbridge had become a Roman town with a trading community that had grown up around the forts, though much less is known of its later history. The raised, stone-flagged floor enabled the circulation of air, which kept the grain cool and dry.

Corbridge *Corstopitum* 👣 Detour 4.1 miles ⊢ NY 982649

■ There has been a church on this site for 1,300 years. The first, a Benedictine abbey, was built by St Wilfrid, Bishop of York, using materials from nearby Roman ruins, probably the fort at Corbridge. In Norman times it was replaced by an Augustinian priory but the nave was rebuilt in the early 20th century. It is now the parish church of the town of Hexham.

Hexham Abbey 🥾 Detour 7.5 miles ├ NY 935641

■ The fort is situated in the parkland of Chesters House, an estate bought by Nathaniel Clayton in 1796. His son John Clayton is the single most important figure in the history of the preservation of the Wall. He excavated Chesters and many other sites, and the museum, shown here, was built in 1896 to house his collection. In the foreground are barrack blocks.

Chesters *Cilurnum* 🥾 30.3 miles ⊢ NY 910703

■ The tranquil park-like appearance of the fort with its close-cropped turf is misleading. In Roman times this would have been covered with roads, masonry and wooden structures, and bustling with people. This photograph looks across the remains of the Headquarters Building towards where the Vallum, a broad, flat-bottomed ditch flanked by a pair of banks, ran parallel with the Wall as an extra defence. Unlike Corbridge, which is situated on the Stanegate, Chesters is one of 16 forts situated directly on the Wall.

■ In Clayton's museum stands the statue of the goddess Juno Regina, consort of Jupiter Dolichenus, a cult that originated in Syria and was popular in Britain in the 3rd century. She is often shown standing on a heifer.

Chesters *Cilurnum* 👟 30.3 miles ← NY 910703

■ Looking East towards the river North Tyne. Two barrack blocks are separated by a central roadway. They are the only barracks from the 2nd century to be seen on the Wall. One barrack block would house 80 infantry or 64 cavalry (who had more equipment). At the far end is a square room for the officers.

Chesters *Cilurnum* 🥾 30.3 miles ⊢ NY 910703

■ The bathhouse stands outside the fort above the river North Tyne. Water was brought into the fort by an aqueduct system. Effluent from the baths and latrines ran into the river. There would have been a civilian settlement around the bathhouse and around the bridge that spanned the river almost opposite the bathhouse.

■ The wall of the bathhouse changing room, with seven niches that are likely to have contained statues representing the days of the week. An altar to Fortuna found on the site suggests that it was here that men passed the time playing games of chance as they relaxed and socialised. These are the best preserved baths along the Wall and, in their size and complexity, confirm the importance of personal hygiene to officers and men garrisoned in the fort.

Chesters *Cilurnum* 🥾 30.3 miles ⊢ NY 910703

■ The Wall crossed the river on a substantial stone bridge. This is the abutment of the second bridge built on the East bank opposite the fort. The arrowhead-shaped opening in the stonework is where the pier of the first bridge stood. The first bridge with at least eight arches was built at the same time as the Wall (AD 122–4) and probably carried the Wall across it. The second narrower bridge had only four arches but was wide enough for a chariot to cross.

Chesters The bridge 🥾 29.6 miles + detour 0.5 miles ⊢ NY 914701

■ A phallic symbol carved on a stone on the Eastern abutment. These symbols, found in many places along the Wall, were a totemic Roman device to ward off the 'evil eye' and be a good-luck charm. Stones with carvings were always the first to be looted, but there are many in the museums along the Wall, especially in the large collection in the Museum of Antiquities in Newcastle.

■ Stones from the East bank abutment after their excavation, which had been started by Clayton before 1860. At the time he started to excavate the Wall, he was a practising lawyer, and was town clerk of Newcastle during its period of major growth.

The work was done by his assistant William Trailford and his son. They excavated the forts of Housesteads and Carvoran, and also rebuilt long stretches of the Wall, which became known as the 'Clayton Wall'.

Chesters The bridge 🥾 29.6 miles + detour 0.5 miles ⊢ NY 914701

■ Near the remains of the Roman fort, Brocolitia, is the Mithraeum, one of several temples along the Wall devoted to the cult of Mithras, an Eastern warrior god of Persian origin associated with strength and the power of good over evil, and popular

with soldiers. Discovered in 1949, in a drought, this is the third Mithraeum on the site. The concrete posts are in place of the original wooden pillars that would have supported the roof.

■ Three altars faced the congregation. This one incorporates slits through which the light from lamps would have created a dramatic effect in the darkness of the windowless temple. This is a replica, the original is in the Museum of Antiquities.

Chicken bones from ritual sacrifices and an ordeal pit in the vestibule were also found. The pit, large enough for a man to lie full length, was possibly for an initiation ceremony involving burial. The Mithraeum was eventually destroyed and abandoned.

■ The sycamores are on the site of the milecastle. Between the forts there are milecastles at intervals of about 1 mile (1.6 kilometres). These are small rectangular forts with two gates. A garrison of 30 to 50 men controlled the traffic through the Wall. There are 79 milecastles along the Wall.

Between each pair of milecastles there are two equally spaced observation towers or turrets.

Milecastle 34 🥾 36.7 miles ⊢ NY 817706

■ Looking East, back towards the sycamore clump. The course of the Wall is to the left of the road (B6318) and runs through the site of the milecastle. The Vallum ran between the Wall and the road. As well as a defence it also provided a communication route between the forts on the Wall.

■ The Hadrian's Wall Path National Trail runs through the wood that borders the slopes of the Sewingshields Crags.

Sewingshields Wood 🥾 37.3 miles ← NY 811703

■ Looking East towards Sewingshields Wood. This milecastle has no North gate as the slope beyond the Wall is so steep, and it may have been more of a watch-tower with lodgings for auxiliary troops. It ended its life in the Roman period as a metalworking centre, and in mediaeval times was the summer sheiling or shelter of a shepherd and his family. The Wall reappears to the West of the wood. It is the Narrow Wall on Broad Wall foundations and it may have been rebuilt in the 3rd century under Septimus Severus.

Milecastle 35 37.6 miles ⊢ NY 805702

■ The Wall curls across a magnificent landscape, though William Hutton who walked the Wall in 1801 at the age of 78 – and walked to and from Birmingham to do it – described it, 'a more dreary country than this in which I now am can scarcely be conceived. I do not wonder it shocked Camden'. William Camden and Robert Cotton visited here in 1599, but had to break off their survey because of bands of robbers, moss troopers known as the 'Busy Gap Rogues'. Stones from the Wall were used to build this field wall, which stands on the Wall's foundations. In the distance, to the left, is Housesteads, the Roman fort of Vercovicium.

■ The late Roman gateway in the Knag Burn valley is flanked by two small guardhouses. This is one of only two gateways in the Wall that are not part of forts or milecastles.

■ The Wall here is now a dry-stone reconstruction by John Clayton. It descends into the Knag Burn valley where the gateway is hidden from view, and then rises to join the outer wall of Housesteads.

Knag Burn 🥾 39 miles ├ NY 791690

Looking back at the Clayton Wall and the Knag Burn gateway. In the foreground are the towers either side of the North Gate, which had arches supported by the central pillar. This gate provides an opening through the Wall itself, but the road outside the gateway was abandoned in the 2nd century when the approach became too steep after roads within the fort were relaid. It may be that it was then that the Knag Burn gateway was built.

Housesteads *Vercovicium* 🥾 39.4 miles ⊢ NY 790688

■ The 'place of able fighters' is the most complete Roman fort in Britain. It was garrisoned in the 3rd century by the First Cohort of Tungrians, a tribe from Belgium. There were civilian settlements to the South of the fort but, once payments from the imperial authority came to an end in AD 407, most of the population would have left. In the Middle Ages Housesteads was the headquarters of a family of border cattle thieves and, as late as the 17th century, it was owned by the infamous Armstrongs of Grandy's Knowe. By the beginning of the 18th century, they had been forced to sell up and some had emigrated to America.

Housesteads *Vercovicium* 🥾 39.4 miles ⊢ NY 790688

■ The granaries (*horrea*), looking East. The stone pillars supported raised floors on timber joists, which kept food dry and vermin free. Grain was stored in sacks and meat could have been kept here as well. These granaries are good examples of the evolution of buildings in forts along the Wall. First, there was a single, wide hall; then it was divided into two parallel halls. Finally, in the 3rd century, this, the North hall, was abandoned. It is difficult to appreciate the organic nature of these settlements when the visible remains may only represent the last stage of their evolution.

Housesteads *Vercovicium* 🥾 39.4 miles ← NY 790688

■ The latrines in the South East corner of the fort. Water, stored in a tank, flowed through a deep sewer to the left and right of the central platform and washed the waste through a duct under the fort wall. The sewer would have been spanned by seats of stone or wood. The stone containers on the platform held sponges applied with sticks from which comes the saying, 'the wrong end of the stick'. The shallow gutter carried water for washing the sponges.

Housesteads *Vercovicium* 🥾 39.4 miles ← NY 790688

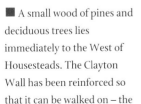 A small wood of pines and deciduous trees lies immediately to the West of Housesteads. The Clayton Wall has been reinforced so that it can be walked on – the only stretch of the Wall where this is permitted. It is now thought that soldiers did not patrol along the top of the Wall.

■ When the Hadrian's Wall Path National Trail opened in May 2003, it became possible to walk the entire length of Hadrian's Wall for the first time since the fifth century.

Housesteads Wood 39.6 miles – NY 786688

■ Walkers enjoy a picnic and a glass of wine.

■ The Wall hugs Housesteads Crags. This is close to where the Pennine Way strikes off North between Cuddy's Crags and Hotbank Crags, having shared the path with the Trail from Thirlwall Castle, 8 miles (13 kilometres) to the West. 15,000 men from three Roman legions were employed to build the Wall. It was built in roughly equal sections of 5–6.2 miles (8–10 kilometres).

Housesteads Wood 🥾 39.6 miles ⊢ NY 786688

■ These are the remains of the North Gate, built from massive stone blocks with parts of the arch now restored. It is now thought that the height of the Wall was not less than 3.5 metres and not more than 4 metres and that this arch may have supported a tower. At a later date the gateway was filled in partially, possibly because this route through the Wall was little used since the ground drops away to the North.

■ The Wall climbs 'the nick without a name' between Housesteads Crags and Cuddy Crags. This is another example of the Clayton Wall, protected with turf.

Housesteads Crags 🥾 39.9 miles ← NY 784687

■ Looking towards Crag Lough from Hotbank Farm. The Wall runs along Highshield Crags up to 60 metres above the water.

■ With its marshy northern bank tucked under Highshield Crags, Crag Lough is one of the most dramatic features of the Trail. The rugged landscape provides a natural defence to the North. The Vallum runs through flatter land to the South.

Crag Lough 🥾 41.2 miles ⊢ NY 765679

■ The most photographed sycamore tree in Britain has been used as a symbol for the Hadrian's Wall Path National Trail. In the 1991 film *Robin Hood: Prince of Thieves* Kevin Costner as Robin Hood rescues a small boy from the tree. This is reconstructed Wall with a new paved path for walkers that goes through a gap in the Wall. Near to the tree, archaeological digging has revealed the original, undisturbed Roman Wall seven courses high.

■ Looking East along a field wall towards the crags. To the North, beyond a ditch that ran parallel with the Wall and was another form of defence, are farmsteads set at regular intervals, which would originally have been sheilings for shepherds guarding the sheep that still graze on the uplands in the summer months.

Peel Crags 🥾 41.9 miles ⊢ NY 756676

■ A steep descent into the gap, with a good view of Peel Gap Tower, a turret or tower, only discovered in 1986. It lies between turrets 39a and 39b in an unusually long stretch of over 700 metres. The remains of many turrets have disappeared because they were demolished in the Roman period and the stones left behind were used for rebuilding the Wall in the 19th century.

Peel Gap 🥾 42.2 miles ⊢ NY 754675

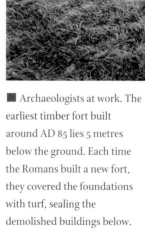

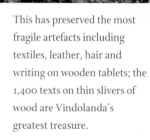

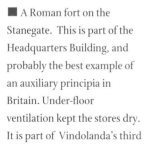 A Roman fort on the Stanegate. This is part of the Headquarters Building, and probably the best example of an auxiliary principia in Britain. Under-floor ventilation kept the stores dry. It is part of Vindolanda's third stone fort, which followed five earlier wooden forts, and was built to house the Fourth Cohort of Gauls in about AD 212. It remained in commission until near the end of the Roman occupation, around AD 400.

Archaeologists at work. The earliest timber fort built around AD 85 lies 5 metres below the ground. Each time the Romans built a new fort, they covered the foundations with turf, sealing the demolished buildings below. This has preserved the most fragile artefacts including textiles, leather, hair and writing on wooden tablets; the 1,400 texts on thin slivers of wood are Vindolanda's greatest treasure.

Vindolanda 42.2 miles + detour 1.8 miles ⊢ NY 770664

■ SPQR. 'Senatus Populusque Romanus', 'The Senate and the People of Rome'. A modern memorial to the Roman army units at Vindolanda. The Tungrians came from Belgium; the Batavians from the Rhine delta; the Nerviorum were cavalry recruited from the Nervii tribe in Belgic Gaul; the Gallorum, originally from Gaul, had served the Roman army in places as diverse as Bulgaria and Algeria.

■ The Ordnance Survey triangulation pillar marks the highest point on the Hadrian's Wall Path National Trail, 1132 feet (345 metres). As an engineering feat, the building of the Wall was not equalled until the canals and the railways were built in the 18th and 19th centuries.

■ The rebuilt wall showing the central core of rubble bound with mortar and the facing of dressed stones. It is possible that, in places, the face of the Wall was rendered, and scribed with false joints and painted white – very different from our traditional image of the Wall.

■ Another part of the rebuilt Wall protected by turf. The Clayton Wall can be distinguished from the original Roman Wall because it is a dry-stone wall without mortar. But later restorations also use mortar. The Clayton method allows the core to breathe, but will collapse if walked on.

Windshields Crags 👣 43.1 miles ⊢ NY 739675

■ Looking down on the Wall as it follows the edge of the escarpment, with the wooded Cawfield Crags (top right). The Romans built the Wall, always taking advantage of the natural features of the landscape.

Thorny Doors 🥾 44.2 miles ⊢ NY 722668

■ In spite of the exceptionally cold water, this disused quarry is used for scuba diving training. It is also the site of a popular car park and picnic area. In 1907/8 a Roman watermill was discovered nearby, with the remains of millstones, possibly used for grinding corn for the garrison. There is no trace of it now.

Hole Gap and Cawfields Quarry 🥾 44.6 miles ⊢ NY 713666

■ A small fort of which little remains except the outline of the walls. This pillar with its carving of a jug is an original altar (not a replica) and stands in the East gatetower. It is the one of the few carved stones still standing along the Wall. Visitors leave coins for luck.

■ Towards the farm the Wall has almost disappeared, reappearing in places as banks of rubble and field walls. The path descends across rough moorland.

Great Chesters *Aesica* 🥾 45.4 miles ⊢ NY 704668   **Walltown Farm** 🥾 46 miles ⊢ NY 683668

■ Near the farm, windswept trees on a little knoll make a much photographed landmark.

Walltown Farm 🥾 46.2 miles ⊢ NY 680666

■ Looking West over a disused quarry, which covered 40 acres until it was closed in 1978. The viewpoint at the top of a steep cliff is one of the most dramatic on the Wall.

■ A motte and bailey castle built in the 12th century with stones from the Wall. It was converted into a fortified hall house between 1330 and 1350 by John Thirlwall who had taken the name 'Thirlwall', which is Old English for 'gap in the wall', when he bought the land. It has been a derelict shell since the 17th century, but has only been open to the public since 2002. The Pennine Way, coming from the South, joins the Trail here and then runs Eastwards to Cuddy Crags.

Thirlwall Castle 🥾 48.2 miles + detour 0.2 miles ⊢ NY 660662

■ West of the village is one of the most impressive stretches of the consolidated wall up to eight courses high with the Broad Wall foundations up to two courses high. During the late 18th and early 19th centuries Gilsland was a spa resort as fashionable as Bath or Harrogate. It was here in 1797 that Sir Walter Scott proposed to his wife, Charlotte. The sulphur springs smell of bad eggs, and the waters of the Irthing which flow through Gilsland are permanently black with peat. The Romans had also recognised the beneficial effects of the water, and an altar found in the 17th century referred to the health of the empress.

■ A Roman bridge crossed the river Irthing – its course follows the line of the trees. The Broad Wall (3 metres wide and built of stone), which starts in Newcastle ends in Willowford. West of Willowford the Wall was built of turf with turf milecastles and stone turrets. The turf Wall was later replaced with a stone Wall.

■ All that remains of the Roman bridge across the river Irthing is the abutment. As the course of the river shifted to the West, one end of the bridge was left some distance from the river bank. Masonry from a late stage in the development of the bridge shows the cut-outs that would have accommodated dovetailed clamps of iron set in lead.

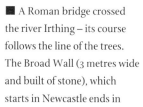

■ It would have been difficult for the Romans to build the Wall without local supplies of limestone to make mortar, and coal to fire it. Most of the stone was quarried, cut and taken to the site on sleds drawn by horses.

Towards Birdoswald 🥾 51.4 miles ⊢ NY 618664

■ In 1858 Henry Norman added this mock mediaeval tower and Gothic style porch to an eighteenth century farmhouse on a site that has been populated intermittently since the Neolithic period.

Roman occupation lasted almost 300 years until AD 410. In front of the house are the foundations of twin granaries of a major fort, as at Housesteads. Around AD 350 the granary nearest to the house was dismantled to repair the granary in the foreground. Later, a wooden hall was built on the foundations. Then a second larger Dark Ages wooden hall was built over the site, a 'princely hall' of the kind described in Anglo-Saxon literature. The modern posts mark the position of its main timbers.

Birdoswald *Banna* 🥾 51.7 miles ⊢ NY 615663

■ Banna was a Roman fort on the Wall. The Wall forms the Northern boundary of the fort and then runs West, bound by the road and a farm fence. The earlier turf Wall, no longer visible, ran through the middle of the fort. When the fort was extended, the turf Wall was demolished but it continued on either side so that the fort straddled the Wall like Chesters. The line of the turf Wall runs through the field to the left.

Beyond Birdoswald 51.9 miles ⊢ NY 612662

■ Pike Hill signal tower was built under Trajan. It is not square with the Wall and a kink in the direction of the Wall shows that it predates it. When the road behind was built in the 19th century, much of the signal tower was destroyed. It is an important viewpoint over the surrounding countryside and was part of the earlier Stanegate communication system.

Pike Hill Signal Station 🥾 55.6 miles ⊢ NY 577648

■ St Kentigern's (or St Mungo's) Church in an idyllic setting stands outside the village down a grassy track, overlooking the river Eden. It was built in 1740 on the site of a 12th century church and was restored in the late 19th century. On the South side there is a simple porch. In contrast, far right, the more generous porch of St Mary, another 12th century church, in Beaumont, a hamlet to the West, also on the Eden. The Wall went through the site and the Normans used stones from it to build the church.

Grinsdale 🥾 73 miles + detour 0.3 miles ⊢ NY 372580

Beaumont 🥾 74.7 miles ⊢ NY 348593

■ The King Edward I Monument on the Burgh Marsh, on the Southern edge of the Solway Firth. Edward I, the 'Hammer of the Scots', died of dysentery on the Burgh Marsh in July 1307 while waiting to cross the Solway Firth to do battle with Robert the Bruce in the ferocious Border Wars. The Monument was restored by the Earl of Lonsdale in 1876 and its inscriptions make it as much a monument to his restoration as it is to one of England's greatest kings.

Burgh-by-Sands 🥾 76 miles + detour 1.27 miles ⊢ NY 326609

■ With no trace of the Wall West of Carlisle, walkers turn their attention to more recent monuments like this house described as 'a farmhouse with panache'. In 1539 John Leland wrote that it had been built on the ruins of an older house, and had been built with stones taken from 'the Pict Wall'. In the year that he died Edward I granted a licence to crenellate the earlier building which is why it is called a castle. The imposing stone steps replaced wooden ladders that could be pulled up if invaders threatened.

Drumburgh Castle 🥾 80.2 miles ⊢ NY 266598

■ The West end of the Wall. Without any visible remains of the Wall or of Maia, the Roman fort, this modest wooden hut represents the official end – and beginning – of Hadrian's Wall. The inscription on this side is in English and Latin: 'Welcome. The End of Hadrian's Wall Path'. On the far side: 'Wallsend 84 miles. Good Luck Go With You'. To the right are the sands of the Solway Firth.

Bowness-on-Solway *Maia* 🥾 84 miles ⊢ NY 225628

■ The remains of the railway viaduct that crossed the Solway Firth, that was demolished in 1936, having been damaged by ice in 1934. It linked the Cumberland coalfield with the Lanarkshire ironworks, and was also used by locals who walked across it in search of a drink on Sundays when Scotland was 'dry'. The cooling towers of Chapelcross Nuclear Power Station, opened in 1959 and now decommissioned, can be seen through the left hand arch. They were demolished in 2007. Hadrian's Wall has survived so much longer than these remnants of our recent industrial past.

West of Bowness-on-Solway 🥾 Detour 1 mile West ⊢ NY 212627